Master Your (Be)ing

Master Your (Be)ing

DR. MICHAEL BERKLEY 33°

The Minister of Numerology

Copyright © 2023 by Berk Entertainment
All rights reserved. This book or any portion thereof
may not be reproduced or used in any manner
whatsoever without the express written permission of
the publisher except for the use of brief quotations in
a book review.

ISBN: 978-1-956174-44-1

Printed in the United States of America

Introduction	1
Begin, You Must	5
Point of Zero-Time	9
From Whence Cometh YOU???	13
Those WHo Walked Before YOU!!	18
War of the Mind	22
Imagine an Antenna	25
The Negative Vibe	30
Osiris's, Negative Green?	35
Electric & Magnetic	39
3rd Eye	42
Invited by OES	45
Invited to Church	54
Vetting Process	65
Len's Decision	71
Len's 1st Reading	77
Len's Ankh Ceremony	90
Master This	102
Conclusion	108
Appendix	116

Introduction

We have entered a new age. We have left the Pisces Era and fully transitioned into the Age of Aquarius. With this transition, the minds are quickly elevating. The problem I see is most people don't know their individual self. Understanding who you are is key to the current way of the world. It is an important element to self-preservation.

Self-preservation is a term often used when describing a person's first natural right. Self-preservation basically is your right to protect yourself from being harmed, in any manner. God gives this right. Several people claim that it can never be taken away.

However, let's examine the words preservation and self before we proceed. The word preservation comes from the word preserve. One of the definitions for preserve is to maintain (something) in its original or existing state. The word self describes the quality which separates a person from others, especially when considered from the perspective of self-examination or reflexive actions. With the concept of self-preservation being a God given right, it now appears to have a different meaning.

The meaning I'm referring to is the topic of this book. The concept of self-preservation is the same concept as the Egyptian saying "know thyself." In the process of knowing yourself, you must know the original you. What do I mean by the original you? I'm referring to the "you" who left the spiritual realm and entered this physical one.

Many of us never truly took the time to find out about our original selves. Instead, we have been swamped with a go along to get along reality, as prescribed by society. We miss out on our true talents and don't know our purpose for being here. We may not even realize that we came here with some baggage.

In uncovering who we are, I will utilize the first science taught by different schools of thought. This science was once known as arithmetic. Although we learned arithmetic in school, this arithmetic is different. It uses the same quantitative methods, but we will be looking at the qualitative meaning of the numbers. The current practice of this arithmetic method is called numerology.

The basic practice of numerology gives us our life path, soul number, outer personality, and destiny. These areas have different labels. In fact, I changed 6 labels in this book. In a similar manner, I will be touching on different areas less spoken of in the basic practice.

By using numerology, we can dispel sayings like "awaken the creative you," "you are a high priestess," or "you are a leader." These sayings may or may not be true to who you are. We can tell your natural rhythmic frequency with numerology.

I will also examine and challenge the trendy topics currently being used for self-awareness. Some of these topics are new, and others are being misused.

So, if you're ready to get to work, let's begin...

Begin, You Must

Imagine the earth rotating around the sun in a counterclockwise direction. A day passes each time it fully rotates on its axis which takes approximately 24 hours. It takes 365 ¼ days of these 24 hours to complete its cycle. The earth has completely rotated around the sun, beginning a new year. This year is different.

A momentous day has been announced. This wonderful day is YOUR arrival. YES, YOU!!! Your arrival has been planned ever since your mother found out she was pregnant.

It is time. The day has arrived. The creative force known by many as God has gathered portions of its energy. This portion, limited, and collective energy is you. The creative force gives you the sign to depart. You prepare for your descent to the earth. You're ready to make the journey to your new temple.

You've been given permission to leave. 10, 9, 8, 7, 6, 5, 4, 3, 2, 1, you take off like a shooting star. You know your destination, although it's not your final destination. You are excited to be sent on your new mission.

Simultaneously, your mother is in agony. She anxiously begins the delivery process. Her pain is unbearable, but she has put in her mind that her miracle must appear. She pushes, and the new temple which has progressively developed within her for 9 months starts to move. It positions itself to move through the tunnel. First the head appears, then the shoulders, and lastly the new soles of the feet are seen.

The doctor grabs the temple by its feet, holds it upside down, and smacks its backside. As the backside is slapped, the temple's boney gate opens in shock, not knowing what is going on because prior to the gate opening, the invisible shooting star swiftly entered one of the two accesses (nostrils). Upon entrance, the shooting star quickly began examining the temple. It had a choice, to continue the journey or abandon the mission.

The star accepts the assignment within the new temple. The middle of the temple inflates. The new star and temple begin their new partnership and prepare to make their collaborative announcement to the world. The center deflates as the gate swings open (your mouth). Then with a new and powerful vibrating sound a cry is heard throughout the room. Everyone rejoices.

The point of entrance into the temple is your zero-time reference. From this point on in your physical life, you start your walk on a clockwise journey. Since the earth continuously rotates in a counterclockwise motion, and you rotate in the opposite direction, friction is created causing your physical body (temple) to begin its aging process.

As all this is going on, you must still progress towards why you are here. You must learn and remember that you are on a mission. Hopefully, you learned the exact mission early in life. If you didn't learn about it, it's not too late. There's a secret to finding your what, how, and why. You find this Secret by moving with the counterclockwise motion of the earth, leaving your matter existence and becoming antimatter. If you don't know how, you're in the "rite" (right) place. I will walk you through the process...

Point of Zero-Time

On the special day, your soul entered your body (the temple), and an energy reaction occurred. An invisible explosion happened. It was released and heard by the physical ear. It was your first cry.

This was the day that the earth stood still for you. It was the briefest moment. It was the point of your zero-time reference. Prior to entering your new temple, you were not affected by what we call time, which is calculated by the earth's motion around the sun. Time began for you when you entered your physical body. Other humans recognized your beginning, initially when your head appeared, but realistically when you first cried.

Yet, something like a chemical reaction occurred. This occurrence was unseen and unheard by the other humans. It can best be explained as a boulder dropped into a body of water. There would be a large splash like an explosion. Then a ripple effect of several circles would follow, in other words small circular waves would be seen.

In your case, when your soul entered the door of your temple, energy was released into at least three directions. One direction filled your body. The other two directions or double current of force curved outward from your mouth. This was a positive and negative stream of energy. Eventually the energy magnetically pulled back together, forming what can be described as the closed part of a circle. A great picture of this moment is the ankh.

Ankh

Where your soul and earth infuse is the point where the horizontal, vertical, and upside-down tear drop shape come together. The horizontal line represents earth's counterclockwise motion. The vertical line represents you. The tear drop represents the chaotic energy coming together with order.

From the point where the circle first came together, it will cross again, forming another circle again and again for your entire physical existence. Your energy forms crossing waves like tachyon energy. The flowing energy moves between two poles or capacitors. You are the resistor controlling the flow of energy. A great picture of the energy movement around you is the Hermes Medical Staff.

Hermes Medical Staff

You are the staff in the middle. The snakes represent the two forms of energy. The wings remind us of the ever-flowing energy. Everything moves (vibrates) at a rhythmic pace (frequency).

Since you, the SOUL, entered your temple (body) on this special day, we know what you are here to do, how you vibrate, and why you are here. We don't know how your mind works yet. This can only be known by the calculation of your given name.

From Whence Cometh YOU???

The beginning point of knowledge has truly never been found. However, a great society once lived at the center of the earth's land mass. The country is now known as Egypt. Egypt is known for its pyramids and temples. It's even been documented that the famous Giza Pyramids are the earth's balancing points between two vortexes. These vortexes are the Bermuda Triangle and the Dragon's Triangle (Devil's Triangle).

The Egyptians completed a lot of amazing feats. Modern day scientists still can't explain these feats. However, everything mysteriously works. Some of the information about how the sciences work has been passed through the generations.

The information has been passed on by way of mythology to some and history to others. So let me share a creation story with you. It begins with a God name Atum also known as Re. Atum thinks about creating other gods. Atum releases the soul creating Shu and Tefnut. From Shu and Tefnut comes Geb and Nut, and from them comes Osiris, Isis, Set, and Nephthys. The ending god spoken of in this group is Horus (Haru/Har). The 9 Deities from Atum are called the Ennead.

Atum's thoughts and acts are recorded by the Deity, Thoth also known as Tehuti. Tehuti is called Hermes by the Greeks, Romans, Jews, and Christians. These groups claim Hermes is responsible for two writings still in use today, the Kabbalah and Kybalion. The Kabbalah has 10 points called the Sephiroth whereas the Kybalion has 7 laws.[1]

The 10 Sephiroth of the Kabbalah ranked, in descending order, are:

---

[1] (10+7= 17) The number 17 represents the Star of the Magi and immorality.

- Keter (the crown)
- Chokhmah (wisdom)
- Binah (intuition, understanding)
- Chesed (mercy) or Gedulah (greatness)
- Gevurah (strength)
- Tiferet (glory)
- Netzach (victory)
- Hod (majesty)
- Yesod (foundation)
- Malkut (sovereignty)

There is an 11th unseen point called Daath which is quite close to the name Thoth (Tehuti). The 7 laws of the Kybalion are:

- The principle of mentalism.
- The principle of correspondence.
- The principle of vibration.
- The principle of polarity.
- The principle of rhythm.
- The principle of cause and effect.

- The principle of gender.

Subsequently, these 2 books have been used to make people phenomenally successful. The books are mainly known today as Jewish Esoteric books.

I want to revisit the story of Atum because of the name Re. Re is another name for the sun. The sun is the center of our galaxy (the Milky Way). The sun is also considered a star.[2] Therefore, Atum's Re is Atum's soul. Atum sent his soul. Atum's soul has laws and principles which can be called universal laws and universal principles.

A part of Atum's soul is continuously sent. You are a part of Atum's soul. You are sent from the spiritual realm to the physical realm to accomplish something great. Atum needs you to complete the mission. You are important piece of the process.

---

[2] I suggested that you are a star earlier.

Atum has been called by different names depending on the cultural practice. Some of the names are God, El, Yahweh, Allah, Adam, and even atom. Atum and Tehuti are truly relevant today. Following this pattern of thought, YOU come from, and are a part of, the Most High Atum.

Those WHo Walked Before YOU!!

Our temple comes from our parents. This is a known fact. Our parents had parents. And the process can be traced back to the original being who some say is the female name Lucy.

We call our family who walked before us our ancestors, if they have transitioned out of the physical realm. Our ancestors are responsible for our DNA. DNA holds an exceptionally large amount of information. There are claims that one DNA strand holds billions of units of information. This means years upon years of information are stored within our DNA.

Examining the DNA and thinking about our ancestors, this could easily mean information is missing in more modern times. Especially, if our ancestors weren't exposed to things. For example, if no one in your immediate lineage were business owners. This would mean that the knowledge of how to operate a business is missing. Another example can be no one was a doctor. Then you are also missing information about health and wellness. The missing elements would make a person think that they must work harder to gain this information.

Analyzing this with my own life, I asked how this could be true?

I based my question on my life's journey at that moment. None of my family members were known to be a part of the esoteric organizations, which I was a member of. Don't get me wrong, some things felt quite natural to me, for instance, being an Army Soldier. My father, my two grandfathers, and a great-grandfather served in the military, making me a 4th generation soldier. Other than this, my life's direction pointed in a different path.

When I uncovered the hidden science, I found out why I engaged so heavily in the esoteric way of life. The science fit me perfectly, so perfectly that it was a little terrifying. Yet, I wanted to test the science on other people to see if it really worked.

One of the people I tested the science on became my student. He was put in the system, becoming an orphan until his biological grandmother got custody of him. Prior to sharing knowledge with him about his true self, he would often get in trouble in school and with law enforcement. After I began sharing information with him, it was like he had a DNA explosion. He saw things differently. He already had an incredible work ethic. In like manner, influential people gravitated to him as if he swallowed a large magnet. He knew several people on his mother's biological side but did not know anything about his father. To this day he is extraordinarily successful and keeps adding to his accomplishments.

The particular science is real, and it has little to do with your ancestral pool. It has more to do with the day you arrived in this physical realm and the name you were given at birth.

War of the Mind

The DNA strands within the temple are like signs, symbols, patterns, angles, and pictures. They have outward and hidden meanings. The worthiness of these things depends on how deep your soul goes into understanding the strands of each DNA. Regardless, you are in a new place and must learn the functions of the temple. It's like the movie released on July 25, 2014, called "Lucy." There is a point where she uploads information about the world. Again, you have this same experience when your soul enters your new dwelling but in reverse.

At the same time, you are still here to complete your mission. So, hopefully your parents understand you were sent for a purpose or reason. Unfortunately, many parents do not understand this. Therefore, you are quickly taken off the path of your mission.

You are guided in a direction which may be unrelated to what you need to do. If this is the case, you, the soul, begin to experience chaos. Regardless of how chaotic your experience is, you begin to upload your new experiences into your temple's cells which lodge into the DNA. This chaotic information will be passed on to your future children.

Subsequently, you will learn and play by the rules that your parents play by. You will naturally challenge some of the rules, only to be confronted with a disappointing response. Your soul knows that this is not you. But the new rules will be beaten into you, physically, mentally, and/or spiritually.

These 2 occurrences put the mind in conflict. First you are learning about the history of humankind based on the lesson taught by way of your DNA. Then, you are being kept away from your mission to follow the house rules. For you, it is war. You're being exposed to 2 fronts at the same time. History has shown that fighting 2 fronts at the same time is nearly impossible.

So, your soul becomes weak. You put up the best fight in which you know. With each hit, water is being thrown on you, canceling your fire (burning desire). 18 years of this treatment is a long time. Your subconscious mind, which is your soul, has gone through a constant ritual, making your experiences new habits. Now you're lost and unsatisfied. You have forgotten who you are.

Do you find your way back? Or do you go with the flow?

The choice is yours.

Imagine an Antenna

It has been taught and written that the earth has several energy grids. The grid lines are several streams of energy moving in different directions. Some call these ley lines. In some areas where the grids cross path, there are extremely dangerous radiation points. The radiation has been given names like negative green.

To offset the radiation, structures like pyramids, mounds, temples, mosques, and cathedrals have been built over the spots. They are built in such a way that they offset the energy and power of the negative green which flows in a vertical direction. The structures ultimately bring harmony to the surrounding area. Without this harmony, there are cases of physical, mental, and spiritual energy which is extremely unhealthy.

In a similar manner, these structures act as antennas, receiving messages in the form of energy from the heavenly bodies. An example of these antennas are the pyramids in Giza, Egypt. The 3 pyramids are aligned perfectly with 3 stars of Orion Star Belt.

The most spoken of the 3 pyramids is called the Great Pyramid. Inside this pyramid, 2 chambers have been located called the Queen's Chamber and the King's Chamber. There is a 3rd chamber considered to be subterranean. The subterranean chamber reflects the chambers above or as the saying goes "As above; so below." The pyramid is said to absorb the invisible energy coming from the heavens and eject the energy from earth. The energy moves in a clockwise or counterclockwise flow.

This is a crucial part, especially knowing that initiations have taken place there. People have received favorable and not so favorable messages in the pyramid. Some of the messages have driven people crazy, to the point of transitioning out of the physical realm. Those who transitioned probably weren't prepared to engage in the initiation. It happens. Not everyone is supposed to receive certain information. It is not their mission. Just because you've heard of things, doesn't mean that you need to participate in the activity.

You like the structures, receive messages all the time. You too are an antenna. Some of the messages you pick up and some you ignore. The major difference between the structures and you are, the structures are fixed, and you are movable. The structures are situated in a position where energy flows to them.

You on the other hand don't attract energy, as taught in the law of attraction. You move into energy streams that freely flow. You are not attracting anything. You are harmonizing with the rhythmic pattern of the energy as you move around. This harmony aligns with your frequency at the time. You are like an adjustable magnet. Thus, it is up to you to be conscious of your frequency through monitoring your emotions or feelings as best as possible.

I often ask my students as we walk by a large body of water, what does that remind you of? They normally are confused. So, I add the statement think of the law "As above; so below." What does this body of water, now, remind you of? They typically do not have a clue.

I go on to explain, the creative force has placed things in our physical realm which are like the invisible or spiritual realm. The large body of water is a replica of the energy field. Water flows back and forth or ebbs and flows. This is what the invisible energy grid does. By this time, they usually agree.

I further explain as we roam around, we should do our best to be like surfers. A surfer will sit in one spot for several minutes waiting for the right wave to ride. We should keep ourselves open, waiting to ride the right energy wave, before we make a crucial decision. In fact, there are energy streams that go good with you but horrible with others. We are not all the same.

The Negative Vibe

Unfortunately, the unhealthy negative green energy has spiked with modern technology. The release of this energy is recking havoc on the environment and the human body. I learned about negative green by reading about Biogeometry, a science discovered by Dr. Ibrahim Karim. According to Dr. Karim, BioGeometry is, "The science of establishing harmony in energy quality exchange between biological fields and their environment, through the use of a design language of form, color, motion and sound."

What is negative green you may ask?

As shown below, there is a sphere of colors. In between the black and white, we are used to calling this the gray area.[3] However, it's also called negative green.

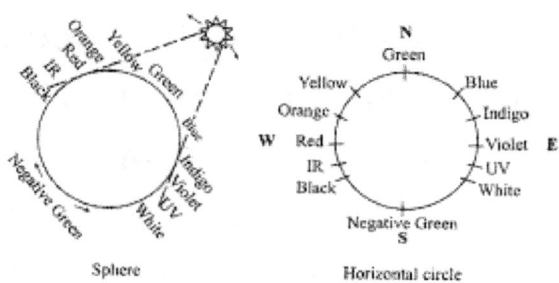

This is an electric and magnetic frequency. The horizontal movement of negative green is friendly whereas the vertical movement of negative green is unfriendly.[4]

It should be known that energy must be offset, especially when something unnatural is created. This offsetting process is considered to be balanced. However, balance usually means an equally even distribution. Yet, the offsetting

---

[3] Have you ever been told to stay out the gray area?
[4] Think of the Matrix movie, where green numbers are flowing up and down (vertical).

doesn't necessarily have to be even. It simply must be present.

You may think that there needs to be equal positivity to balance the negativity. However, negativity can be offset by more negativity in a different direction. It should be known that positive and negative have other meanings than just good and bad. It can also mean aggressive and passive or active and inactive. Now-a-days, people call it masculine and feminine (law of gender), which I argue is the worse way to explain this phenomenon.

Once again, negative can be offset by another negative dynamic. This is seen when the vertical negative green is offset by a horizontal negative green. In Biogeometry, high harmonic of ultraviolet and high harmonic of gold are added to the horizontal negative green to further offset the vertical energy. This shows that vertical negative green is potent. These frequencies occur in the spiritual realm but affect the physical realm. This negative green adds on to the negativity that we already experience.

The color patterns are partially used when explaining chakra energy in the human body. The color is simply the speed or vibration of a frequency (energy), which produces the color we see. These energy patterns are affecting us. Many of us don't know the extent of this effect.

Your mission is based on energy as well. Certain energy radiates more with who you are than other energies. As I will explain later, your energy has an opposite energy effect. This does not mean it's positive or negative. It simply means it is.

First, you must understand there is only one of you. You don't have a higher and lower self. You simply have a self. This self-fluctuates between every situation or event. You are being affected at a degree, but you are not the degree itself.

To get a better understanding, I'll use the concepts of temperature and speed. The temperature changes (effect) based on different events (causes). There are not 2 temperatures. There is 1 temperature at a specific degree. In addition, there are not 2 speeds. There's 1 speed according to how fast or slow you are going. Again, there is only 1 you.

Osiris's, Negative Green?

I've heard and read several stories about the Egyptian Deity Osiris. A twist to the story entered my mind while learning about BioGeometry. So, I'll revisit the story, giving the twist.

Reexamining the diagram, we see green is at the north, red is west, violet is east, and negative green is south. Black is in the southwest position, and white is in the southeast.

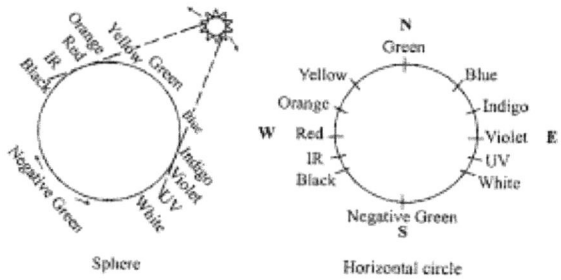

In pictures of Osiris, he sometimes appears to be green. In brief, the story goes that Osiris was the ruler. His brother Set became jealous of him and assassinated him. Set disposed of Osiris body.

Osiris' wife, Isis located the body. With knowledge received from Re, she was able to heal the body to a certain extent. Then she got pregnant and gave birth to Horus. Horus grew up and sought revenge against his uncle, Set. In the battle, Horus lost his left eye. He regained his eye, from Tehuti.

If you want a more complete story, there are several versions written. I want to explain it using the above picture. I wrote earlier of Atum giving his soul (Re). Atum's Re is white. Before the tragedy of Osiris, he was under the sun of the north as green. Set is like the sunset, so he is represented by black.

When Set assassinated Osiris, Osiris turns to negative green. The negative green position aligns with the storyline that Osiris was over the underworld. Since he was lost, it took Isis and her sister Nephthys to offset the negative energy which was released because of his death. Isis and Nephthys representing the high harmonic of ultraviolet and high harmonic of gold ultimately offset the negative energy, when they joined forces with the horizontal negative green of Osiris.

Further, I'll explain my concept on Horus. Horus lost his eye because of his out-of-control ego. Although the story speaks of the eye, it seems to refer to the function of the brain. Thus, his ego was in the left-side of his brain. The left brain is known to have functions like logic and analytics. The right brain is considered the creative side.

Horus' logic was misplaced. He sought revenge for the wrong reason. He had to sit at the feet of Tehuti to regain his eye. Tehuti gave him universal knowledge which is the knowledge of how things really work. This information was absorbed in Horus' right brain.

The duties of each side of the brain are important for you to understand what hemisphere of the brain you are in, when you are processing a thought. The brain shifts to each hemisphere throughout the day. There are times that you seem to forget something. More than likely, your brain is functioning on its right side. I'm saying this to say, it's normal to forget occasionally.

Ultimately, I'm convinced the Ancient Egyptians were leaving messages for us. These messages were instructions on the power of the energy, which is flowing throughout the earth, and how energy affects us.

Electric & Magnetic

As shared, harmful negative green travels in a vertical (upward) direction. It travels from the earth. Energy also enters the earth's atmosphere from the planets, moon, and stars. These heavenly bodies do not explain who you are. Instead, they indicate how certain energy streams affect you.

The closest body to the earth is its moon. The earth and moon's orbital rotation causes a gravitational push and pull motion. It's said to ebb and flow twice in 24 hours. The effect is mostly recognized with the sea levels. Subsequently, the sun also has a gravitational effect along with the other planets and stars.

You are like a magnet being pushed and pulled by different energy forces. Depending on when you entered the physical realm, you can tell what type of effect the heavenly bodies have on you. This is found in the esoteric science of astrology. When you entered your temple, your body was located at a specific place and was aligned with the bodies in heaven.

In astrology, there are 12 sections called houses. Each house has a focus. The planets fall at a certain degree somewhere within one of the houses, when it comes to you. Again, you are not a degree, you are AT a degree. Once again, the planets are pushing or pulling you. They are not explaining who you are. They explain how you may act in certain situations.

Like the earth, all accept one of the planets in our galaxy rotate counterclockwise. The only planet that rotates clockwise is Venus. It is rotating in the same direction as the so-called time. Venus is the 2nd closets according to astrology. Venus is the planet of love. Since it's such a small planet, and it goes against all the other planets, it's no wonder why people have a problem with love. Venus (the green planet) is at odds with the other planets.

Then there are tarot cards. People pull tarot cards to explain what is going on with you. There are several distinct factors to this art. One is the meaning of the pictures on the card, especially the geometric symbols. Another is the relationship between the person pulling the card and the event or person involved. A tarot card more than likely will change if you ask the same question or are seeking an answer, a second time. This is because energy is fluid. It is constantly moving.

Both methods can be dangerous, if done and/or explained by an amateur. These sciences are nothing to play with. In all things, caution must be taken. So be careful to whom you listen.

Additionally, each person who is not on their mission can be a source of negative green. Yes, you too can be poisoning our environment.

3rd Eye

Before switching gears to explain how to discover your true self, I want to revisit the current you. As stated, prior, when you entered your temple, you had to learn the signs, symbols, angles, and meanings of the information imprinted in the DNA strands left by those who walked before you. This imprint becomes part of your reality. In other words, your soul (subconscious mind) learns the reality of those who walked before you, and their reality becomes your soul's reality.

As you are learning your new dwelling, you are also being influenced by the outside world, mainly your parents or guardians. These influences add-on to your reality and may conflict with what is within your temple. You begin to question what is, now, the old information, which the bible calls, "the old man," that you learn about from the DNA and the current or new conscious experiences.

Your conscious experiences eventually win. The new experiences, when done repeatedly, replace the old information, making the old information dormant. In other words, new experiences become habits. Each time something is done over and over again, it becomes habitual. The new habits can run into difficulty when exposed to the broader influences of the outer world.

When you attempt to make logic of the outer world, you base your logic on things you already experienced. Thus, the process is based on what you already accepted as logic. Here again lies possible conflict because what you know to be true doesn't fit with the actions of the outer world. So, you do your best to adjust to get a clear understanding.

In this adjustment, you may be introduced to esoteric information. A common concept when seeing and thinking you understand something which is occurring, is the opening of the 3rd eye. Some people claim that it is an art of being aware of or seeing what is going on around them. They claim to have a great ability to see the bigger picture.

In my experience, the 3rd eye has nothing to do with being aware. It is an art used in the process within the science of visualization and imagination. When you close your eyes, a screen like a movie screen can appear. Then you may be able to see pictures. This is a science that can change your life. It can replace an unwanted reality with a more desirable one. This is another gift given to us by the creative forces where we can gradually shift the energy from the unseen, slowing it down, degree by degree, until it manifests in the physical realm.

Invited by OES

I was invited by a group of Eastern Stars to explain how to unravel the many messages secretly hidden in the form of symbols and words throughout their system. The person who invited me had read one of my co-authored books written over a decade ago. We wrote about the planet Venus and its connection to the inverted 5-pointed star.

If you stand on earth and look at the movement of Venus around the sun, it moves in a certain direction which the Eastern Stars would be familiar with. The complete pattern takes approximately 8 years. It travels in a geometric pattern which looks like an inverted 5-pointed star. We also made mention that another name for the planet Venus is Lucifer.

I will present more information about the planet Venus later in this section. However, I started the discussion speaking of the 7 Liberal Arts and Sciences. The arts are logic, grammar, and rhetoric. The sciences are arithmetic, geometry, music, and astrology. My focus is on the first science which is arithmetic.

Arithmetic has an exoteric and esoteric property. The exoteric practice of arithmetic is quantitative. While the esoteric practice of arithmetic is qualitative. I use both. I use the quantitative method to find the value of all numbers involved, by combining all the numbers in an equation whereas I use the qualitative method to explain the meaning of the final value.

The system of arithmetic that I'm using is called numerology. The science of numerology is the study of numbers which have energetic and rhythmic influences on our lives. The method I use most to interpret the influence(s) is the Rule of 9. The Rule of 9 is also known as Pythagorean

Numerology and modern numerology. This is a number system which utilizes the numbers 1 through 9. Numbers higher than 9 are reduced by adding the numbers together to get a single digit, unless it is what's known as a master number (11, 22, 33... 99). A single digit is known as a natural number, and compound numbers are multiple numbers (10 and higher).

Sometimes, I use Chaldean and Gematria numerology. Typically, when I see the numbers 23, 37, 51, and 65, I am alerted to the Royal Star system found in Chaldean Numerology. In like manner, when I see the number 26, I think of the number of God from the Gematria system. All the systems expose a lot.

In the 3 systems I've mentioned, there are letter and number equivalents. A basic search about numerology can give the needed information to understand the significance of their relationships. I don't want to spend much time explaining the letter and number equivalence. I want to show more of it in action.

After you spend some time studying numerology, you may come across things like this. There are 7 months with 31 days. There are even 31 versus in the first book of the bible and Genesis has 7 letters. Or the name Solomon has 7 letters which equal 31. Is this a coincidence or could they all have similar meanings?

The number 7 can mean mysteries, rest, and/or revealing. Whereas 31 reduces to #4. The #4 can mean stability, the foundation, physical realm, persistence, building, destroying, and many other things. The #31 is also a mirror reflection of the #13 which means transformation. However, 30 is a divine #3 because the #0 comes after it. The #3 represents creativity. Yet, the #10 advances the #3 ten times. The #10 means Wheel of Fortune. It can also mean Wheel of Misfortune, depending on the circumstances. Each number has opposite extremes. 10 is a higher frequency than the #1. The #1 is individuality, leadership, etc.

Let me revisit the planet, Venus. In coauthoring the book *Do Freemasons Worship Lucifer*, we challenged the notion many people have. They automatically think that Lucifer is the devil. Once again, Lucifer is another name for Venus. Examining the name Venus, it equals 18 (4+5+5+3+1= 18). 18 represents chaos and conflict, because the #1 and #8 are in opposition of each other (1 is positive while 8 is negative, or 1 is negative while 8 is positive). 18 reduced equals 9 (1+8=9). The #9 represents universal love, completion, and even the bigger picture.

Venus is also a 5-letter word which has a cornerstone, a keystone, and a capstone. The cornerstone is the letter V. The letter V is the 22nd letter in the English alphabet. The #22 is a master number which means the master builder, when used improperly it is the master destroyer.

The keystone is the letter that holds things together or an anchor. Only odd number words have keystones. In Venus, the keystone is the letter N. The letter N is the 14th letter. This can mean a person's foundation is on a much higher level than normal, but because 1+4= 5, the person needs to be willing to change for their own freedom and/or adventure.

The last letter of a word is the capstone. Therefore, Venus' capstone is the letter S. The letter S is the 19th letter. This can mean the prince or princess of heaven. Reduced the #19 is the #10. In this case, 10 is considered a hidden number. It again means the Wheel of Fortune. Then the #10 reduced equals 1 (individual, leader, etc.).

The cornerstone, keystone, and capstone tell us a lot. For example, the planet, Venus, is the planet of love. Thus, when approaching love, we must handle it like a master who is building the most beautiful structure. What will hold the building process together is a strong foundation. Upon successful completion, we will possess and feel like the prince or princess of heaven. But it will be difficult because all the other planets rotate around the sun in a counterclockwise direction. While Venus rotates in a clockwise direction. There's a lot of energy going against it.

I went on to explain that numerology can tell each person their purpose of being here, what they are here to do, how they are vibrating, the way they think inwardly and outwardly, and how a harmonious mind can give a great gift. I explained how your birthday is fixed and your name is mutable because you may take on a nickname or get married and your last name changes.

Additionally, numerology can show us if you didn't fulfil a mission in your past life. This is called a Karmic debt. This debt will be repaid in this lifetime, consciously or unconsciously. No matter if you attempt to avoid it, the universe will collect. There are so many more things that we can figure out about a person using numerology.

Before, I took questions, I added another technique which I call the LEVEL Number (others call it the balance number). I used the acronym of the Order of Eastern Stars which is OES. O is the 15th letter, E is the 5th letter, and S is the 19th letter. When adding the compound numbers, we get 39. The #15 is a number associated with the occult. In this case, I explained that the SiStars are alchemists who changed through initiation to be princesses of heaven.

In like manner, the natural numbers are O (6), E (5), and S (1). This equals 12. 12 is associated with the 12 zodiac signs. 1+2= 3. In some schools of thought, the #1 is the father, #2 is the mother, and 3 is the child. This equation is also known as a+b=c, relating to a triangle. The triangle is said to be the strongest geometric shape.

I ended the lecture with a few questions and was asked if I could be contacted to do numerology readings.

Invited to Church

A few weeks later, I was invited by a group of young people to accompany them to a debate. The debated was against their former pastor. They recently came across information which challenged what they were taught. I agreed to attend the debate. I explained that I would not say which side was right or wrong until I heard both arguments. I did not share my thoughts about most pastors being more aligned with Christolatry than students of Christ's instructions. However, I further explained I would present information that the group may have overlooked because of their new findings.

It started off as a heated debate. Then it was my turn, I asked what the term is for interpreting the bible. No one knew. So, I asked one of the group members who invited me to look up the word. It's called hermeneutics.

I then asked someone to read Genesis 1:27, "***So God created man in his own image, in the image of God created he him; male and female created he them.***" I asked what is a human who has both male and female gender? The intellectual and sarcastic scholar who supported the pastor blurted out hermaphrodite. I agreed.

Next, I spelled the words hermeneutics and hermaphrodite. I asked if they saw any similar letters between the two. Someone answered the letters "herm." I agreed. Then I took the word hermaphrodite and separated it into three sections (herm-aphro-dite). I explained that I was taught this technique nearly 3 decades ago.

The pastor and his followers weren't interested. But the group led by a young lady were attentive. I explained that I would add, subtract, and change letters around. Herm became Hermes, Aphro became Afro, and "dite" became deity. I wrote Hermes, the Afro or

African Deity who is Tehuti. The Greeks called Tehuti, Thoth before they called him Hermes.

Next, I told them that I would use two main characters of the bible along with numerology. The characters would be Moses and Jesus. But before, I used them, I wanted to show them that numerology was used in the bible. I spoke of the book of Genesis. Genesis (7.5.5.5.1.9.1) equals 33. From Genesis 1:1 to Genesis 2:2 there are 33 verses. Genesis 2:2 speaks of the 7th day of creation. Removing the colons from 1:1 and 2:2, we see the numbers 11 and 22. 11, 22, and 33 are considered master numbers. The #33 is the master teacher or master lesson. The #22 is the master builder or master plan. The #11 is the master inspirer or master motivation.

I continued by explaining the story of Moses. Moses was taught in Egypt. He left with his people, after convincing the pharaoh to let the people go. The pharaoh only agreed to let

Moses' people go, after God brought a curse to his house. When Moses led his people out of Egypt, the pharaoh had a change of heart. The pharaoh commanded his soldiers to chase and capture Moses. Moses was stopped because of the Red Sea. Yet, God gave him the power to split the Red Sea. Moses' people were able to walk on dry land. When the pharaoh entered, the sea closed and supposedly ended their lives.

This is an allegoric story. I will show you why. The 5-letter name Moses (4.6.1.5.1) equals 17. 17 represents immortality and the Star of the Magi. The name Moses also has a capstone, keystone, and cornerstone. The cornerstone is M, the keystone is S, and the capstone is S. The letter M is the 13th letter. 13 means transformation. 4 is building, stability, or foundation. 6 is community, family, or responsibility. 1 is leadership, originality, or individuality. 5 is change, adventure, or freedom. Moses would do something for his people, holding things together because he was considered the leader, and completing the task in a magical way becoming like one of the memorable stars seen in the heavens.

Reducing 17 (1+7), we get 8. The #8 is a number which represents God, karma and infinity. In fact, 8 is shaped like the infinity sign. When Moses split the sea, it was split into two sides like the 2 circles of the #8. One was the conscious mind and the other was the subconscious. Moses separated what the people knew which was the way of the Egyptians (subconscious) from what they were going to learn (conscious) which was to cross over or Hebrew.

For 40 years, they struggled in the wilderness. So, Moses went to speak with God. While speaking with God, God gave him some tablets. The people became impatient because Moses did not return when he claimed he would. Aaron attempted to redirect their impatience by telling the people to give the women's and children's gold to him. He asked specifically for the women's and children's possessions to induce the men to remember why they were following Moses, in the first place. Aaron then molded a golden calf.

Upon Moses' return, he saw the people worshipping a golden calf. The acts of the people infuriated him. He made Aaron destroy the golden calf, making the people eat the gold. What was happening is the golden calf represented the Age of Taurus (bull). They were entering the Age of Aries (ram). They were changing eras like we left the Age of Pisces for the Age of Aquarius. This story explains how people have difficulties going from the old ways of life to the new ways.

The tablets he destroyed were the writings of the 7 laws. This was expertly written in Genesis 2:2 (the verse of the master builder [22]) as the 7th day of creation. The day God rested, in other words laid the universal instructions. Today, these 7 laws are found in the book called the Kybalion. The 7 laws or principles of the Kybalion are:

1. The Principle of Mentalism
2. The Principle of Correspondence
3. The Principle of Vibration
4. The Principle of Polarity
5. The Principle of Rhythm
6. The Principle of Cause and Effect
7. The Principle of Gender.

Eventually Moses returned to speak to God. This time God gave him another set of tablets with the 10 commandments. What we know as the 10 commandments are a disguise of the 10 sephiroth (sefirot) or tree of life in the Kabbalah. The 10 sephiroth are:

1. Keter, the Divine Crown
2. Hokhmah, Wisdom
3. Binah, Understanding
4. Hesed, Mercy
5. Din, Justice
6. Tif'eret, Beauty
7. Neza, Eternity
8. Hod, Glory

9. Yesod, Foundation
10. Shekhinah, God's Presence in the world

Both the Kybalion and Kabbalah were written by Hermes who again is the African Deity, Tehuti.

The 10 sephiroth are really the story of the Egyptian Gods called the Ennead (Atum; his children Shu and Tefnut; their children Geb and Nut; and their children Osiris, Isis, Set, and Nephthys) and Horus (Osiris and Isis' son). In both the Kabbalah and the story of the Ennead, there is a hidden figure. The Kabbalah's hidden figure is Daath whereas the Ennead's hidden figure is Thoth (Tehuti). Daath and Thoth are phonetically similar.

Using the Rule of 9 Numerology system, the Kabbalah equals 20. 20 is the awakening or reawakening. The Kybalion equals 35. 35 can mean that God is changing something, by way of an adventure, to gain its freedom. 35 is reduced to 8, which again is the number of God. Thus, the esoteric meaning of Moses' journey is he had to go back to what he knew worked. He traveled in his mind to remember the teachings of the Egyptians. There's no need to forget the basics when starting something new. Universal laws don't change. As the bible says, "God has no favorites" and "there's no new thing under the sun."

I jumped straight into speaking about Jesus before any questions were asked. The 5-letter name Jesus also has a cornerstone, keystone, and capstone. The letter J is the cornerstone, S is the keystone, and S is the capstone. It is like the name Moses, except for the letter J. J was once known as a master number. It is the 10th letter of the alphabet. Jesus equals 11. He is the master inspirer, prepared to give motivating or inspiring lessons like a master.

As we know Jesus is the son of God. So, I explained the connection to the Ennead story. When Atum created Shu and Tefnut, the first word he spoke was HW (pronounce HU). Therefore, HW is the soul of Atum. The soul is known as a sun (son). The Egyptian Deity who represents the sun is Re. Thus, Atum's Re is Atum's Sun (soul) like Jesus is God's son (sun). Even the word atom and Adam are offshoots of the name Atum.

I ended with using the King James Version Bible because it was translated from the Hebrew language. We can find the Hebrew translation to English in the James Strong's Concordance. In the translation, it's obvious the bible can't be taken as literal as the English language reads. Even the acronym KJV is coded. K is the 11th letter, J is the 10th, and V is the 22nd. Together it equals 43 (4+3= 7). However, the level number tells me that an initiate is elevating from a master inspirer (11) to a master builder (22). It can appear that the initiate is walking between 2 pillars (K/11 & V/22) for higher knowledge. So, there's no need to dismiss the bible completely. It should be studied for its esoteric meanings.

I didn't tell them that King James is known as the 1st in England and the 6th in Scotland. I see the number 16. The 16th tarot card shows a tower being hit by lightning. Two people fell out of the tower. This means information can hit you like a bolt of lightning destroying the way your subconscious and conscious mind think. The #16 reduced is 7. Again, the #7 means the mysteries, revealing, and rest. It all makes sense if you look at things differently.

Vetting Process

The same young lady who led the group at the church debate called me for a numerology reading. Before I started, I had to vet her. So, we had a conversation about what she was looking for and what she could expect of me. I found out that she first heard me at the Eastern Star gathering.

Two things I look for first are the day of birth and the signature name, which is the name a person normally goes by. She was born October 30th, 1997. From her birthday, I knew she was vibrating on a #30 frequency. This is 3 times 10. In other words, the 3 has the nature of a divine and infinite wheel of fortune.

She also told me that her signature name is Lynn. I spelled the name to her. She corrected me, spelling her name LEN. The name Len (3+5+5= 13; 1+3= 4) doesn't align with her day of birth, 30th, according to the 8 different trinities in the magical square sequence.

1	2	3
4	5	6
7	8	9

Magical Square

The 8 trinities are as follows:

1-2-3

4-5-6

7-8-9

1-4-7

2-5-8

3-6-9

3-5-7

1-5-9

As shown the #3 and #4 are not in any of the sequences. So, I knew Len had issues in her life. I would normally tell her to change her name for a better alignment, but we didn't agree to work with each other at this point.

Len told me that she already received a numerology reading, but it was unclear and didn't answer her questions. I explained to her that just because she receives a numerology reading, it doesn't mean that it is absolute. She must work to live up to the numbers she is given. I gave her an example of possibly having leadership numbers in her chart. The numbers are there but as energy continues to flow, she would have to enhance the quality for it to be effective. In other words, she would have to learn the different aspects of leadership. Because the leadership qualities which worked in the past, wouldn't work today. Therefore, she would have the right number to make a great leader, but she must do the work. Len understood.

I went on to tell her that I developed a system that is slightly different than the ones she would normally come across. I use the same mathematical techniques, but I switched the titles to make it more relevant with what is currently trendy. Instead of looking at a person's name for their soul, outer personality, and destiny numbers, I replaced the soul with the subconscious mind, the outer personality with the conscious mind, and the destiny number with the superconscious mind. In other words, my position is the importance of the mind and how they relate to each other. I consider that when the conscious mind and subconscious mind work together, they are gifted and more aligned with the superconscious mind. In like manner, instead of just looking at the life path number based on the date of birth, I examine people's purpose (reason, why) they are here, how they dominantly vibrate, and what they are here to do (mission).

I go deeper into numerology to find hidden messages. There are plenty hidden messages like one's karmic debt from a past life. This debt will be repaid during this lifetime, typically within the productive years. The productive years are found by a specific method. Everyone's productive years don't start or end at the same time.

There's not a one-size fits all answer. We can have the same natural numbers in our whole chart, but if the compound numbers in our name are different, this can change our experiences. Our experiences can also be different depending on where we live as in our country, state, city, and even street address. Numerology is an intense science.

I also told Len that if we work together, we can do a basic reading or we can go back to her zero-point reference. If she wants a zero-point reference, I would be the Grand Master of Ceremony. I would walk with her through her journey, but she would have to be honest with herself to get the best result. She would need to reflect on her life to analyze if things she did were already explained with the numbers in her chart.

I told her that I had to be real with myself, as well. When I learned the numbers in my chart, I had to take time to get to know my real self. For me, everything made sense in both successes and failures.

Len told me that she wanted to do a zero-point reference reading. She also expressed wanting to know why her life is the way it is. I explained to her that we would go through 3 stages in her process. She accepted and shared her full maiden's name and birth date with me.

Len's Decision

With a zero-point reference reading, I first need her full maiden's name and date of birth. Her full name is Helen Ruth Garrett and date of birth is October 30th, 1997. Since she was an Eastern Star, she possessed information not known by the masses. How much information, I didn't know.

I told her that I would contact her soon for an appointment. Until then, I would work on her chart. She accepted.

I often worry about if someone is on a path that they shouldn't be on. There are many times where people have numbers which aren't for leaders, but they are in a leadership position and are having extreme difficulties. Another incident I've seen is those who have leadership numbers but don't have executive ones. These people tend to only worry about themselves, while they are leading a group of people. The people feel neglected and rebel against the leader.

Additionally, I've seen people who are supposed to partner with someone else but want to work alone. These people wonder why things aren't working out for them. Numbers tell us a lot. Knowing your pattern of numbers can help you avoid misery or gain success.

So, I immediately began working on her chart, first using the Rule of 9 system. I start with the birthday because this is a fixed number. The birth date never changes.

Birth Date- 10/30/1997

10	10	1
30	30	3
1997	26	8
2037	66	12/3

Then I work on the name. We tend to change our names through nicknames, marriages, cultural practices, and other reasons. This is the chart for the Rule of 9 that I'm using.

1	2	3	4	5	6	7	8	9
A	B	C	D	E	F	G	H	I
J	K	L	M	N	O	P	Q	R
S	T	U	V	W	X	Y	Z	

Again, Len's full name is Helen Ruth Garrett. Usually, you'll see the name as follows:

	5		5			3				1		5		19/10/1
H	E	L	E	N	R	U	T	H	G	A	R	R	E	T	T	16 letters
8	3		5	9		2	8		7		9	9		2	2	64/10/1
																83/11

I wanted to go more in depth with her name. So, I separated the first, middle, and last names. The first name gives information on the physical aspects of life. The 2nd name gives information on the emotional element. The 3rd name shares information about spiritual aspects.

		5		5		10/1
	H	E	L	E	N	
8			12		14	34/7
8			3		5	16/7

	3			3
	21			21/3
R	U	T	H	
18		20	8	46/10/1
9		2	8	19/10/1

	1			5			6
G	A	R	R	E	T	T	
7		18	18		20	20	83/11
7		9	9		2	2	29/11

Vowels

1st name	10	10	1
2nd name	21	3	3
3rd name	6	6	6
	37/10/1	19/10/1	10/1

Consonants:

1st name	34	16	7
2nd name	46	19	10
3rd name	83	29	11
	163/10/1	64/10/1	28/10/1

Full Name: Helen Ruth Garrett

1st name	44	26	8
2nd name	67	22	4
3rd name	89	35	8
	200/2	83/11	20/2

Since Len was looking to better her life, I look for Karmic Debt numbers which may be a major problem for her. These numbers are carried on from a past life. You will have to repay this debt, regardless of you being conscious or unconscious of it. The numbers are 13, 14, 16, and 19.

In Len's chart, I see the numbers 16 and 19. Although she has the letter N in her name which is the 14th letter, this doesn't affect her. The #16 is in her first name. The number 19 is in her consonants and total vowels. I will explain it all to her later.

As you saw, when adding her full name together, the final calculation is 11, reduced from 83. However, if I were to look at the final calculation from the vowels (1) to the final calculation from the consonants (1), I would get 2 instead of the master number 11. Therefore, everything depends on the way you calculate the name.

Len's 1st Reading

I emailed Len a recording of my numerology findings.

Greetings,

This is The Minister of Numerology, Dr. Michael Berkley 33rd Degree, sharing my findings with Helen Ruth Garrett, born October 30th, 1997.

I'll begin with the fixed part of the numerology, your birthday. The birth date never changes, while the name can change because of marriage or even a spiritual practice.

The way I will explain this may be unlike the way other numerologists explain numerology.

10-30-1997

Your birthday explains several things. It tells why, your reason, or your purpose of you being here. It also explains your dominant frequency. We can, in addition, gather a broad assumption of the mission you are here to do. This mission can be an individual mission or a skill to be included for a collective mission.

Let's start with what most people ask, your reason for being here, in other words, your purpose in life. We can find this by adding the month and day of your birth.

$$10+30= 40; 4+0= 4.$$

The compound number 40 tells us that your purpose (why/reason) in this lifetime is to do some divine work or build something of a divine nature. The divinity of this number is shown by zero. Your number is 10 times higher than the normal natural vibration. The number 10 is the wheel of fortune or wheel of achievement.

The natural number 4 is associated with words like grounded, foundation, stable, work, building, and persistency. Your purpose is to do some type of work in a stable and persistent manner.

Next, we know your dominant frequency by your day of birth. Again, your compound number is 10 times higher than its normal vibration. Being born on the 30th demonstrates that your imagination is active.

Creativity is the main word the natural number 3 is associated with. Therefore, the energy you give most things will be on some scale of creativity.

The last number we will discuss in this work is what you are here to do. This is found by adding the month, day, and year. There are several ways numerologists calculate this number. I keep the month and day the same, regardless of if it is the 10th, 11th, or 12th. I add the full compound number to the full natural or compound number of the day. Then, I add the year which may come to a double-digit compound number or can be reduced to a natural number. For example, the year 2022 (2+0+2+2= 6) or in your case (1+9+9+7= 26).

The mathematical equation I used was 10+30+26= 66.

There are numerologists who will reduce this 66 to 12 and then 3. Typically, the same numerologists who reduce this #66, only recognize the numbers 11, 22, 33, and occasionally 44 as master numbers. But I recognize the #66 as one of the 10 master numbers.

Master number 66 defines high responsibility as well as high dependability. This is a number showing the mastery of humanistic disciplines. Thus, your work while in this lifetime should be in the level of understanding of the functions of culture or society.

As you may have noticed, I didn't give a specific job or career title. What I shared was a very broad example which gives you many options. Again, this is what you are here to do throughout your lifetime. It isn't who you are, it is what, how, and why you do the work you do.

Therefore, examining your birth, your mission is to become an expert in some form or fashion in the humanity field which improves people. You are not to get caught in tradition. You are to be imaginative with your work.

Now, let's look at who you are. The you I'm speaking of is your mind within the temple that you're occupying while here. We find this by way of your birth name.

Helen Ruth Garrett

There are 16 letters in your full name. One of the meanings for the number of letters is there will be a major lesson every 16 years. There will also be a minor lesson every 7 years. Using the Rule of 9 letter and number value system, your full name equals 83 reduced to 11.

There are 5 vowels and 11 consonants. The vowels in your name equal 19, 10, and 1 whereas the consonants equal 64, 10, and 1.

The vowels in your full name explain the real you, your soul, or subconscious mind. I call the vowels, the vow to El. El is a Hebrew name for God, the creative force. When the creative force sent you to enter your temple, you arrived as a number 19 frequency.

Since you told me that you wanted to know why your life is the way it is, let us get this out of the way. 19 is one of the four karmic debt numbers. 19 shows that you must pay a debt from a previous existence or life. It will be paid if you are conscious of it or not. In your previous life, you misused power. You roamed with secret thoughts, possibly not being honest with those who were under your guidance. This means until you pay for what you did, you will have challenging times and lose a lot.

When you repay it, your life will be fortunate. This is seen when the 1 and 9 are added, equaling 10 (the wheel of fortune). Still, your natural number is the number 1. You think individualistically. However, this is a number representing a leader. According to the ascending and descending energy flow, the negative number of #1 is #8. 8 is known to be an executive. Even though you are a leader, you may have problems guiding people underneath you, which is an issue that is being carried over from your past existence.

You must understand that everyone has freewill. Everyone will not think or act like you. It's clear in numerology that there are at least 9 different characters. During your leadership journey, it is important to remember this.

Your conscious mind is known by the consonants in your full name. This is how people see you. Subsequently, it's how you display what you're thinking. You display the number 1 frequency. Thus, several people recognize you as a leader while others may see you as selfish and egotistical. This is an extension of the real you.

When you combine your conscious mind with your subconscious mind, you receive your ultimate gift. I call this your superconscious mind. Adding 19 to 64 equals eighty-three. 83 reduced equals the master number 11.

#11 represents the master inspirer or master motivator. This master number does things out of the ordinary. For example, instead of giving someone a pep talk, this person may give the other person a new idea.

Again, your superconscious gift is to masterly inspire people in an unordinary way.

I want to make this a little more personal for you. We will do this by using your first name. Your first name gives more information on your individuality.

When adding the letters in the name Helen, they equal 26. 26 in a different form of numerology called Gematria is an important number. It stands for the name Yahweh which means he brings existence into whatever exists. Yahweh is linked to the words Jehovah and God.

However, 26 reduced equals 8. The number 8 represents karma, infinity, an executive, and God. I will bring in your signature name at this point. You are known as Len. Len equals 13 and 4.

Both the names Helen and Len can cause much confusion, conflict, disharmony, and sickness because they aren't in agreement with your birth date of 30/3. I suggest that you use a different signature name. A suggestion is to spell Len, Lynn. Lynn equals 20/2. 2 is in the 2-5-8 trinity of numbers with the number 8.

The name Helen has a cornerstone, keystone, and capstone. The cornerstone is the first stone laid when building a building. In your case, the letter H is your cornerstone. H is the 8th letter. You have the capability to approach things in an executive manner. This offsets some of the number 1 energy you have. The keystone is the stone which holds things together. It is also known as the anchor. The letter which holds things together for you is the letter L. L is the 12th letter in the alphabet. With #12, 1 is active and 2 is passive. Together they equal 3 which is their creation. Another way of looking at this is your father (1) and mother (2) created you. You hold things together by being creative. This aligns with your day of birth. Therefore, the 30 has assistance.

The capstone is the ending point or last act of an action. It also explains the attitude in which you have. Your capstone is the letter N. N is the 14th letter. 14 is reduced to 5. 14 gives a person the freedom to do the necessary work to change the individual's foundation. The number 4 is known to be the negative number to 1. Both are connected to the sun. Negative does not always mean bad. It can also mean passive, inactive, or grounding. The end of projects or goals will likely change the way you, as an individual, look at or do things.

Now if you ever feel out of balance, the initials of your full name are the letters which will level you out. As you know, your initials are H, R, G.

$$8+9+7= 24; 2+4= 6$$

The number 6 equates to family, community, and responsibility. Therefore, you may think about what's best for your family or community. You may even remember that you are responsible for your feelings or act.

Since, I mentioned your family, the last thing for this reading that I will look at is your family name. This is the tribe of people who you are connected to.

The 7-letter name Garrett equals 32. The number 32 is a number associated with words like power, America, and Christ.

32 is 30 and 2. 3+2= 5

Earlier I spoke briefly of these numbers, but this time the 30 is accompanied by 2. This can be seen as the ancient Egyptian saying, "As above; so below." The 2 is the below number meaning partnership or companionship. Therefore, 32 tells us that your family came together to create a powerful change for freedom in an adventurous manner.

Garrett also has a cornerstone, keystone, and capstone. The cornerstone letter G is the 7th letter. 7 represents the mysteries, revealing, or rest. The keystone letter R is the 18th letter. 18 can bring chaos and conflict to the final project. 1 and 8 equal 9 (completion, bigger picture, universal love). Your capstone is the 20th letter T. 20 means the awakening or reawakening.

Examining your last name, it again shows that your tribe engaged in using the mysteries to awaken people which may have caused conflict because it went against tradition or social norms. I spoke of you being here to do something that is untraditional.

Wrapping this up, I have given you a lot to process. Thus, I wish you peace until our next communication.

Len's Ankh Ceremony

The Egyptian Ankh is known to mean the key of life. The question is what is the key to your life?

I will walk Len through understanding her chart in a better way.

Len is still in her formative years. She would not start her productive years until 2031, when she turns 34. The formative years are the 1st of your 3 life cycles. The other cycles are productive and harvest. The formative years are basically when you are learning your environment. You will make many mistakes while attempting to understand things.

While many people call themselves cabalist, I consider myself more of a Kybalionist. Instead of using the 7 principles in the Kybalion, I use 9 principles. My position there are set laws. Although we have freewill, it's better for us to perfect our missions. In working towards perfection is best to study the laws of the universe. By studying them, we can better use them to accomplish our mission.

I emailed Len a picture of a person standing in front of a pyramid, so that she could understand the look I was about to explain. At the entrance of the pyramid stood a lion on each side of the door like 2 pillars.

I began the 2nd recording.

Greetings,

This is The Minister of Numerology, Dr. Michael Berkley 33rd Degree. I will further explain your numerology chart with an exercise. I emailed you a picture, which I suggest you open to let it sink in your mind.

Let us begin. Everything is Mind; the Universe is Mental. This is an important lesson which we should understand. Not only do we have a mind, but our minds came from and are still connected to a much larger mind.

Thus, the greater mind needs our lesser mind to accomplish certain things in this physical world. The greater mind released a portion of itself, sending you (the lesser mind with free will) to experience this current physical realm. Although you are allowed to accomplish your mission of your own free will and accord, universal laws are the laws. They have no favorites. Therefore, I suggest you study the laws and see how your chart and the laws best function together.

If you had parents or guardians who did not understand that you were here on a special mission, it is nearly guaranteed that you were led astray from where and what you are here to accomplish.

Therefore, I want to guide you back to your beginning, that moment you traveled to experience this physical reality. Again, you were sent by the creative force which I call the All. You were released on a specific day, resembling a shooting star sent towards your temple or body.

Your mother began the welcoming process. Her soul gave permission for her temple to release the temple she was forming within. Your head appeared then the rest of the body. The deliverer positioned you to grab your ankles. Soon after, the soles (souls) of your feet emerged into the physical world. You were held upside down, so that your nostrils were facing the heavens. You, as the shooting star, entered your nostrils.

To make sure the arrival process was completed, the deliverer smacks your backside, causing the door (your mouth) of your new temple to open, releasing energy that could be heard by the human ear. In other words, the sound of a cry is heard. The people in the room rejoice. You've are now considered a living soul.

***

For this next part, you need to look at the picture I emailed you. You can either prepare yourself literally or visualize the preparation.

You will need to be in white. White symbolizes ether or energy. You will also need to close your eyes or put a blindfold on.

Being blindfolded is like a seed being placed in the ground. The seed enters darkness before it grows. Therefore, you must also enter darkness, to experience the true and esoteric growth process.

When you are ready, we can begin...

Since your nose is the same shape as a pyramid. We will use the image of the pyramid to represent you entering your body. Now, imagine yourself standing in front of the pyramid with the soles of your feet bare on the ground. Today is the day that you remember who you are.

The pyramid was purposely built to gather energy from the universe including the earth. It is an antenna.

Visualize me standing with you at the entrance of the pyramid. I place your hand on my shoulder, so I can guide you through the door.

When we walk through the door, A loud noise is heard behind you, as if, a large door is slammed shut.

An echoing voice says welcome to your new temple, my princess.

By the vowels in your full name equaling 19, it is well known that you are a princess of heaven. Even though you possess this high frequency, you are not here to give yourself praise or expect others to praise you. You are here to assist humanity. Therefore, you must learn diverse elements of modern society to complete your mission.

We walk again, entering a room. You are told to sit in the lotus position at the altar. I take your hand off my shoulder and help you sit down.

You're asked what you are here to gain. I whisper in your ear "say greater knowledge of self."

You repeat it.

A voice responds: greater knowledge you seek; greater knowledge you will receive.

Your blindfold is removed. You see 9 faceless glowing beings around you. Each represents one of the 9 natural numbers.

A being wearing a yellow robe stands at the high noon position and represents the #3. Standing at the 1 o'clock position, a being wears green and represents the number 4. At the 3 o'clock position, the being wears blue, representing the #5. At the 5 o'clock position, the being wears indigo representing the #6. The #7 being stands at the 6 o'clock position, wearing purple. At the 8 o'clock position, the being wears black and represents the #8. At the 9 o'clock position, 2 beings stand side by side. The 1st is wearing an array of colors, representing the #9. The other is wearing red and represents the #1. At the 10 o'clock position the being is wearing orange, representing the #2.

You feel a breeze moving counterclockwise.

When you first entered your temple, you were only able to make sounds, unable to talk where people could understand you. Therefore, you will not be able to talk or ask questions during this ceremony. We are here to share information that you can absorb, so listen closely. Don't worry how you will remember it because it is already within you.

The **#3** being speaks: On 10-30-1997, the earth's frequency was vibrating on a master number 66. This was a high and unusual vibration. It was a day that humans could master themselves. Their mastery could have been weaved together like the most skillful artist.

Your assignment is to assist humans to transform themselves.

The **#4** being speaks: You must uncover a way to work on a higher level than the average citizen to accomplish this. The reason which is your purpose is for a better structured society.

The **#3** being speaks again: Thus, you will mostly vibrate on a fortunate energy of optimism. You have a strong energy for self-expression. You have the gift of being sociable and a great communicator, being able to effectively communicate with a diverse group of people. You have limitless creative energy.

You feel the breeze change direction. It is flowing clockwise.

The **#7** being speaks: Your task will not be straight forward. You must repay a debt from your past life. You caused your mate and other life partners, great pain. Therefore, you will encounter loss in this lifetime. You will be conscious of your loss. How you manage it will be up to you.

The **#1** being speaks: You also misused power. You have been allotted power in this lifetime; however, you will feel disrespected. Know that this is what you must repay from your past life. Repay it in this life, and you won't carry it into the next.

In order to do this, you must have personal confidence. You must not expect others to do this for you. You must stand alone and rely on your own abilities.

The **#4** being speaks: You must accept responsibility for your own acts. You will have to work for your wants, although you dislike working.

The **#6** being speaks: You will have a difficult time accepting the true value of things. You want a perfect marriage, according to your ideal of perfection.

The **#5** being speaks: If you advance with these ideas, you will not be successful in your mission. You have a great ability to change. If you use this ability, you will be quite successful in your mission. You can accomplish this by analyzing the day and time. Then if you move accordingly, using the power of your mind, you will experience success. You choose.

With that the room goes dark, and you are once again standing on the soles of your feet, outside of the pyramid.

I present you with an ankh. It is to remind you of when you, the shooting star, were sent by the

All to enter your current temple. The horizontal line represents the earth moving counterclockwise. The vertical line represents your temple. When you entered your temple, it was like a splash when a rock falls into water. It creates a circular wave. Thus, the circle is a reminder of when you entered your temple. You release a sound when the positive (1) and negative (2) came together (3), producing a sphere. The sound is the waves.

This ankh is a reminder of this momentous day, in which, the creative force sent you into this physical to accomplish what is needed to be accomplished. The numbers and meanings are the key to unlock the life that you are to live.

As you may have noticed, not all the beings spoke. Only the beings who represented direct numbers affecting you spoke.

We will continue at our next communication...

Master This

In any mastery, the methods are important. The methods are sometimes veiled in wording. For example, the bible states "Love your neighbor as yourself..." This verse is more of a method of instruction than a literal meaning.

When you understand how the mind works, you will possibly see why it's important to love your neighbor like you love yourself. As it's been said, "if you say you can or say you can't, you are right." Where you focus, your mind will follow. Thus, to get a complete love of yourself, you must love others. Your focus is on the act of love not the actual person. Taking your focus off love, takes the focus of love off you as well.

Subsequently Len was given information which shows her normal actions. If she wants to change her actions, she now knows where and what to focus on. She will have to take a deep look at herself to be successful. She was given a cheat sheet.

With this in mind, I began the final recording.

Greetings,

This is The Minister of Numerology, Dr. Michael Berkley 33rd Degree.

Just like a chiropractor realigns the body, you have experienced a regeneration of your original self.

You have been given the tools for self-mastery. When you utilize these tools, you will be harmonized with the energy which aligns best with you.

You must not forget that different energetic frequencies with different rhythmic patterns exist all around you. These energies take on dual properties of being active or passive.

You reenacted the part of a sun known in an Egyptian school of thought as Horus. Your soul

(Horus) was reacquainted (initiated) with the 9 Ennead. You had to lose your left eye just as Horus lost his, during the battle against his uncle Set. The left eye replicates your left brain, the gatherer, where your logic resides. The gatherer moves counterclockwise like most of the planets in the galaxy.

Horus (your soul) had to seek out and sit at the feet (soles; soul) of Tehuti who sent the 9 beings to explain what you needed for self-improvement. Here, your soul began moving clockwise. Your right brain had to be opened. While opened, the motion of expansion was occurring. In this great occurrence, your soul was able to receive the arts and sciences of the universe, which you have been gifted with and resides within your inner self.

Once this most illustrious gift was given and understood, Tehuti replaced Horus' left eye. In other words, the logic of your part of the universe was reawakened in the left brain.

The process is like the part in the movie, "The Matrix," where people would get unplugged and plugged into the system that would take them into the simulated world.

In this case, your 1st brain (reptilian brain) is connected to the pineal gland which looks like Horus' eye. Therefore, in this ceremony, you were unplugged from the pineal gland to receive information. Once you received the information, you were plugged back in.

With this in mind, it's important to stay in harmony with what you were told. You may have heard of Abraham Hick's "Least resistant path?" In the teachings, it's suggested to find that feeling good comes first over anything else. In order to experience joy, you need to train your logical mind to stop thinking about potential problems, obstacles, or worries.

I will add your most dominant frequencies are the least resistant. Focus on the meanings which accompanies your numbers, and you will see much more success as well as accomplish the mission the creative force sent you to do.

Utilize your imagination to visit heaven. Your inner self is heaven. So, take time to travel within, take your shoes off, and rest (7) there for a while.

Again, while you are in heaven, don't forget that you are still a moveable antenna that gets pushed and pulled like a magnetic pole. Planets, the sun, stars, and other earthly frequencies are pushing and pulling you. The beauty of this is that you have free will. Therefore, you should have, what some call, magnetic integrity. Agree with your mission and develop a relationship with the energy which dominates your physical existence. Don't harm others with your powers, and you will go far.

All in all, you have been given your chart. Now go and use it to the best of your ability.

If you have any further questions, you can always contact me for more consultation.

Conclusion

Each of us has a mission in this physical world. Each person is a specific and combined group of energy, gathered and sent, to accomplish the mission for the creative force. In other words, the creative force took parts of self to create you. This makes you limited. You are a part of, not the entirety, of all the energies of the creative force.

Since most of this book is based on the Rule of 9, I will conclude with 9 things to take into account.

1. Play your role

    Focus on what you are here to do. Again, you are a part of the whole. You are NOT the whole. This means there are people who play distinct positions in the grand scheme of things.

2. Understand that astrology and tarot cards do NOT explain who you are as an individual.

   Astrology is the last science of the 4 Liberal Sciences. To measure how planets affect you, you use numbers (numerology) and shapes or symbols (geometry) to understand how the frequency (music) is influencing you. Tarot cards can have an immediate change, if you pick a card asking the same question or even if 2 people pick a card at the same time when asked the same question. Tarot cards depend on everyone's frequency and everything going on in the space at the time. Energy affects people differently. How you feel about something may NOT be how your partner feels.

3. You are using a temple (body) to accomplish your mission.

Your soul needs the temple to operate in this physical realm. The temple has all kinds of secret, let's say, devices left by those who walked before you (ancestors). The DNA of the temple you occupy may not have been activated with the accomplishments of your ancestors because everyone in your lineage was born before the accomplishments occurred.

4. Find your mission.

    Your mission is found by adding your birth month, day, and year. This does not change. However, the meaning of this number is broad. Therefore, each number may be found in almost every successful endeavor of humans' accomplishments. For example, the history of technology has changed throughout time. Humans went from learning to walk, to riding animals, to creating vehicles to carry them. A person with the #5 would be needed to make the change whereas a #4 person would be needed to build or plan the progress.

5. Find your overall purpose/ reason/ why.

    This is also found in your date of birth. By adding your month and day, you will uncover your purpose in this existence. For example, your number could be 3. Your purpose would be to express yourself or create something through the media. On the other hand, you may be a #6. Your purpose would be focused on your family or community.

6. Find your dominant vibration.

    Again, this is your date of birth. It is the actual day. If you were born on the 2nd, you give off a partnership vibe. Likewise, if you were born on the 7th, you give off a sense of mystery.

7. Find the original you.

> The original you or the initial gathered energy is found in the vowels of your full name. I recognize the vowels as your Vow to El. El is a Hebrew name for the creative force. The vowels are considered your soul or what I call your subconscious mind. This is the inner you that can be hidden from the rest of us. With the vowels, we know if you are a natural executive type (8) or if you are a natural leader (1).

8. Find out how you appear to others.

> This too is found in your full name. It is the consonants of your name. I recognize it as your conscious mind. This is what we all see. You can be a #9, showing great compassion for nearly everything. You see the bigger picture or complete picture. So, you could be considered a person who radiates universal love.

9. Find the gift of your minds working collectively.

   Once again, this is positioned in your full name. I call it the superconscious mind. When you allow the 2 minds to work together, you will receive the gift of the creative force. You can more easily accomplish your special mission. If your mission is a #1, and your subconscious is a #3 whereas your conscious is a #7 (3+7= 10; 1+0= 1), your superconscious (1) aligns with your mission (1).

Subsequently, your numbers may NOT align perfectly. You may need to change your name because your birth date never changes. This change will alter the way you think, although the original you still exist. To accomplish your mission, what is needed is the usage of different energy.

You may believe it or not, but this isn't the first time all your energies have been gathered to accomplish something. Therefore, numerologists can calculate any leftover baggage that you need to correct. This is your karmic debt or something you owe from previous existences. It will be collected if you are aware of it or not. As the bible instructs, "God has no favorites."

Remember each number has a positive and/or negative (active and passive) vibration. Each number also has an opposite number. Thus, in one year your life can be excellent, and the next year you can have turmoil. There are times to progress, and there are times to sit still and gather yourself. Your life looks like the movement of a stock on the stock market exchange. The key is to keep yourself out of the red. This is accomplished by building yourself so high that when down periods occur you are way above the foundation line.

I will end by suggesting that you get a numerology reading by a well-qualified numerologist. I'm saying this because the first numerology reading that I received over a decade ago from my elder, Lovell Rowser, made a world of a difference to me. I began studying at his feet soon after this reading. He honored me with the title "Minister of Numerology" and often calls me Brother Insight. So, I suggest that you do yourself a favor and find that qualified person to assist you in finding your right path.

Sincerely,

The Minister of Numerology

Dr. Michael Berkley 33°

contact@berkentertainment.com

Appendix

I copied these meanings of the numbers from two highly recommended books. The first book is *Numerology and the Divine Triangle* by Dusty Bunker and Faith Javane:

> The number 1 represents the male principle, the yang. It is the pioneer, striking out alone, seeking the experiences which will establish its distinct identity. It is in the process of discovering its own abilities. It is raw energy, positive, original, and creative, in a state of perpetual motion. Since 1 is alone and is imbued with so much creative energy, it must decide how its energy will be used. It must take command and have the courage to maintain its direction without fear of opposition.
>
> 1 is the real I AM of humanity, the unity of all, the unit of vibrational measuring. It is self-consciousness.

Keywords: original, independent, aggressive, individualistic, creative, dominant; the first in a series, the start of any operation or activity, the leader, the pioneer, the boss who likes authority. "He who goes forth."

The number 2 is the pair, the duo. It is changeable and adaptable and can also be indecisive. It is the agent, the go-between, the diplomat, and peacemaker, because unity can only be accomplished through a meeting of the minds, a compromise on each side

2 represents the feminine principle of receptivity, the yin, which seeks a union of two distinct entities. It is the gestation period which things begin to form. 2 collect and assimilates. It seeks a balance between opposing forces, and therefore represents cooperation, attachment, and partnership. It

is the peacemaker, with an avid attention to detail. Because 2 is so keenly away of opposites, it has a pronounced sense of rhythm and harmony. Music appeals to its sympathetic and emotional nature. The maternal, patient, and sensitive characteristics of 2 cause it to place others first, before itself. Union is its goal, not separateness; therefore, it is obedient to and understanding of others. It seeks harmony and assimilation above all.

The hydrogen ions which sprang into existence under 1 are no hurtling through space. They will be drawn toward one another by the law of mutual attraction, or the law of the number 2.

Keywords: adaptable, tactful, understanding, gentle, cautious; a follower rather than a leader.

The number 3 combines the qualities of the 1 and 2. It is a fascinating and diversified vibration, carrying the qualities of manifestation and self-expression. The ion, which sprang into existence from 0, sought to assert its individuality under 1 and felt the attraction of others under 2, now awaken to its need for social interaction. 3 is the need to communicate and become involved in the pure joy of living. Through its exuberant response to life, 3 bestows sunny radiance and enthusiasm upon all. 3 is the extrovert whose personal magnetism draws others and inspires them to expand and grow. It is the performer who possesses an innate appreciation of pleasure, romance, art, and beauty. Its creative imagination allows all things to be possible; it therefore becomes involved in many emotions and experiences. 3 is friendly and expansive, thriving on sociability and variety. If any of the numbers could be called happy-go-lucky, it would be the effervescent 3.

Keywords: expansive, sociable, dramatic, communicative, diversified, creative.

The number 4 is stability, a 4-square consciousness, the symbol of law, system, and order. It is firmness, security, stability, and conservatism. It is the builder who must submit to earthly things were form and substance are the predominant elements. 4 is nature and relates to earth. The formation of the earth took place on the fourth day in the biblical story of creation.

The attraction the ions felt under 2 led to interaction under 3. Now, under 4, the inevitable concentration of energies occurs. Formation takes place. The ions realize that they can no longer scatter their energies but must now begin to place them in a productive, orderly system. 4 therefore develops a practical nature, and through self-discipline, binds itself to a conventional routine exercise of its energy.

Keywords: form, work, order, practicality, construction, stability, endurance, discipline.

The number 5 is freedom, change and adventure. Curiosity and constant activity produce a resourceful, adaptable, and versatile entity always ready to take a chance.

Since 5 is the midpoint in the rule of 9 cycle, it allows for decision-making. It might be called the pivotal point in which the ions, now encased in flesh and form, must decide upon their future in the rest of the cycle 6 through 9. It now meets with many opportunities and varieties of experience through which it will be given the information it needs to make the decision.

5 is involved in much superficial interaction with groups and crowds. Because of its past varied experiences, it is the natural promoter and advertiser, fluent in communication, with a little information about a lot of things, and a desire to travel here and there to communicate it. 5 attracts the opposite sex because of an irresistible magnetism, and this attraction sets the stage for the domestic responsibilities which naturally follow under 6.

Keywords: versatility, resourcefulness, adaptability, change, activity, travel, adventure, promotion, speculation.

The number 6 is conscientious; it desires to bring harmony, truth, justice, and a sense of balance into its environment. Love and compassion are uppermost in its mind, and it can therefore be an effective teacher, counselor, or healer. Others are drawn to it because of the understanding which emanates from it.

The ions, under 5, had the opportunity to experience many events and emotional encounters. They are now ready to take a social and family responsibilities, or the 6 vibration. 6 is a domestic and artistic vibration, and, under this number, the ions must adjust to the needs of others.

The 6 desires a close companion, marriage, and a home and family where beauty and harmony prevail. A need for group harmony and service to the community follows naturally. 6 settles down, blending into the conservative element of the community, where it can create better standards of living. Gifted in the arts, it can also express its creative potential through its developed sense of balance and become a fine artist in its own unique field.

Keywords: family and social responsibility, service, love, compassion, counseling, healing, creativity.

The number 7 seeks answers. It tries to establish a philosophy by which to live and attempts to penetrate the mystery behind its existence which it has never questioned to this point. Because solitude is necessary for analysis, the 7 feels the need to spend time alone, away from the crowds, in touch with nature. It looks for friendship with those of an elevated consciousness that can match its own.

And on the seventh day God rested. All things rest under 7 because time is needed in which to think. The ions under 7 feel poised and calm; they realize that they now need to be still and to know. They have established a routine for their energy, and now analysis begins.

7 ushers into the cycle a physical completion without apparent effort. Goals that have been long sought are now magically attained. Spare time is available in which philosophical and metaphysical interest can be pursued. Perfected thinking is the goal of 7, which is philosophers, teachers, mystics, and the clergy come under this influence. The physical facet of 7 also relates to the health of the body which is highly sensitized through this vibration.

Keywords: quiet, introspective, intuitive, analytical, inspirational, reclusive, philosophical, mystical.

The number 8 will assume power, for it now has achieved control and responsibility in its chosen field. Recognition and financial rewards are bestowed, and expansion and growth in the business world take place.

Under 8, karma is king, and the ions will reap what they sown. Power is the quality associated with 8. Ardor, zeal, steadfastness, and the ability to see in broad terms give it the ambition and added qualities needed to achieve material goods. 8 has the drive to overcome all obstacles and eventually to succeed through ability and perseverance. 8 can now go to the very top with the ideas and plans that have been formulated gradually during the last seven cycles. Through fair and ethical standards, good judgement, and organizational abilities, it will achieve recognition, power, and financial wages.

Keywords: power, responsibility, financial rewards, good judgement, recognition.

The number 9 is selflessness and compassion. Encompassing a lover for all, it desires to apply its energy to universal service.

It bestows an impersonal but just view of life, one that is generous, benevolent, and patient. This is the artist and thinker who has developed skills through the preceding cycles and is now ready to share his or her knowledge with the rest of the world.

The ions are in their final state of completion. They have travelled the entire cycle of nine parts, ingesting experiences along the way. Now, in the closing cycle, they reach a total understanding and tolerance of others' views and prejudices.

9 is ready to give back to the universe some measure of what it has learned through the 8 previous steps of the cycle. The law of cyclicity allows for no waste and demands input for output. When this is done willingly, the completion experienced under 9 brings only joy at the gift of life and the freedom

with which to enter the next cycle unencumbered.

Keywords: love, compassion, patience, universality, tolerance, selfless service, endings.

Lloyd Strayhorn's book *Numbers and You: A numerology guide for everyday living*.

NUMBER 1:

Positive: original, creative, leadership, forceful, inventive, ambitious, daring, active, visionary, dynamic, and independent.

Negative: bossy, headstrong, fearful, selfish, bullying, egotistical, dominating, tyrannical, impatient.

NUMBER 2:

Positive: gentle, understanding, artistic, romantic, loving, considerate, tactful, sensitive, persuasive, charming, and a good listener.

Negative: moody, critical, shy, deceptive, changeable, petty, insincere.

NUMBER 3:

Positive: proud, active, optimistic, joyful, creative, ambitious, conscientious, popular, expressive, sociable, and youthful.

Negative: boastful, wasteful, superficial, gossipy, dictatorial, careful, extravagant, scheming.

NUMBER 4:

Positive: practical, methodical, solid, studious, punctual, organized, structured, visionary, different, useful, and orderly.

Negative: narrow, slow, stubborn, moody, spiteful, negative attitude, and indifference.

NUMBER 5:

Positive: traveler, clever, adaptable, freedom loving, intellectual, quick to learn, crisis oriented, flexible, and literary

Negative: vulgar, wanderer, irritable, wasteful, and a tendency to addition.

NUMBER 6:

Positive: compassionate, magnetic, dependable, affectionate, concerned, loving, artistic, responsible, and caring.

Negative: obstinate, dogmatic, stubborn, doubtful, irresponsible, and uncaring.

NUMBER 7

Positive: analytical, silent, intuitive, spiritual, independent, truth seeking, love of nature, knowledgeable, and an authority.

Negative: skeptical, sarcastic, cynical, deceptive, withdrawn, fault finding, nervous, and self-doubting.

NUMBER 8

Positive: determined, powerful, faithful, consistent, practical, capable with money and finance, authoritative, strong willed, and loyal.

Negative: misunderstood, cruel, greedy, morbid, destructive, revengeful, and hateful.

NUMBER 9

Positive: organizer, energetic, dynamic, inspirational, good opinion of self, leadership oriented, daring, universal in outlook, and humane.

Negative: quick tempered, impulsive, day dreamer, narrow minded, combative, emotional, lack of direction.

Both books are filled with a lot of valuable information.

The Tama-Re Book Series on Lulu.com

Children Numerology Activity Books

New but Old thought books on Amazon.com

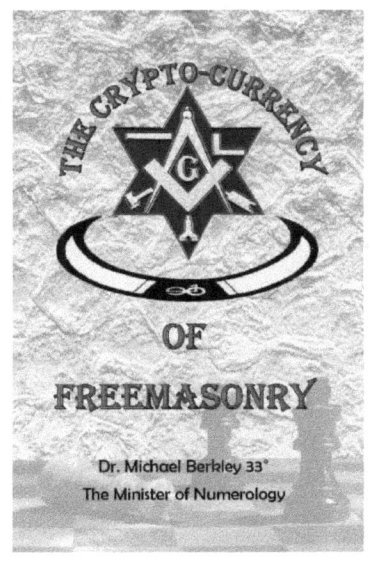

www.ingramcontent.com/pod-product-compliance
Lightning Source LLC
Chambersburg PA
CBHW071215160426
43196CB00012B/2320